So *That's* Operational Risk!

(How operational risk in mortgage-backed securities almost destroyed the world's financial markets and what we can do about it)

Douglas Robertson

Office of the Comptroller of the Currency

OCC Economics Working Paper 2011-1

March 2011

Keywords: Operational risk, financial crisis, mortgages, asset-backed securities
JEL Classification Codes: G21, G24, G28

Douglas Robertson is a Financial Economist in the Policy Analysis Division of the Office of the Comptroller of the Currency, 250 E St. SW, Washington, DC 20219. Please address correspondence to the author (phone 202-874-4745; fax 202-874-5394; e-mail: douglas.robertson@occ.treas.gov).

The views expressed in this paper are those of the author and do not necessarily reflect those of the Office of the Comptroller of the Currency or the U.S. Department of the Treasury. The author would like to thank Michael Carhill, Mark Levonian, David Nebhut, Desiree Schaan, Kostas Tzioumis, and Gary Whalen for helpful comments and suggestions and Rebecca Miller and Morey Rothberg for editorial assistance. The author takes responsibility for any errors.

So *That's* Operational Risk!

(How operational risk in mortgage-backed securities almost destroyed the world's financial markets and what we can do about it)

Douglas Robertson

March 2011

Abstract: We describe the economic crisis that began in the U.S. mortgage market in late 2006 as a consequence of cascading operational failures linked to the securitization process. Operational risks including mortgage fraud, negligent underwriting standards and failed due diligence combined with modern finance to initiate a nearly catastrophic crisis in financial markets and a painful recession.

To avoid a repetition of such a crisis, we propose an asset inspection methodology that employs simple random sampling and direct verification of loan-level information. We describe how sampling can verify critical asset quality information reported in prospectuses for asset-backed securities, and we demonstrate the sampling procedure with a simulation exercise applied to a mortgage-backed security. We also provide a template for reporting the results from the sampling inspection that should become part of a security's prospectus.

It is particularly important that credit-rating agencies adopt the inspection methodology to address a fundamental flaw in their credit-rating process for structured finance, namely, a lack of due diligence regarding asset-backed security vintage verification. The sampling methodology proposed here exposes "liar loans" and mortgage fraud; it applies quality assurance supervision to nonbanks seeking access to the securitization channel, and it should help restore confidence in the asset-backed securities market.

I. Introduction to Operational Risk

The working definition of operational risk among financial institutions is the risk of loss from inadequate or failed internal processes, people, and systems or from external events.[1] Even if you haven't heard of operational risk before, you know what it is. It is fraud, human error, and system failures—to name a few of the many problems that qualify as operational risks. In other words, operational risk is just a relatively new term for some very old problems that on a small scale happen every day in financial markets and typically are managed with little or no incident. Occasionally, however, operational risk explodes onto the scene with dramatic and devastating effect.

One example of an extreme operational risk event is the collapse of Barings PLC in 1995. Even the Barings collapse, though devastating to Barings, was largely an internal and contained event. In contrast, what the world witnessed from the spring of 2006 through the fall of 2008 was a cascade of operational risk events in which an operational failure at one institution or in one market exposed an operational failure at another institution, which in turn triggered another operational failure in an unnerving and destabilizing sequence of accumulating catastrophes. The natural reaction of credit market players who find themselves treading in a minefield of unfolding risk is to stand still, which is precisely what they did in October 2008, which in turn brought the world's credit markets to a near standstill.

---

[1] See Basel Committee on Banking Supervision (2006), p. 144. For example, the operational risks we address in this paper include inadequate or failed verification of loan application information, misrepresentation, and inadequate internal controls. While credit risk addresses the probability that individuals will default on their mortgages, especially poorly underwritten mortgages, the focus of this paper is on the failed internal processes and people, i.e., operational risks, that effectively created billions of dollars of credit risk.

In this study, we follow the sequence of operational failures that brought us to such a standstill. Tracing this sequence, we see how an operational risk in the mortgage industry that is probably as old as mortgages themselves—mortgage fraud—exposed operational failures by mortgage originators, mortgage bundlers, credit-rating agencies, asset managers, investors, and ultimately regulatory agencies. We examine how linkages among these credit market players allowed operational failures that began in the mortgage industry to infect the broader asset-backed securities market, the commercial paper market, and ultimately the credit-default swap market. Mounting losses from these numerous operational failures rapidly depleted capital, undermined confidence even more quickly, and soon led to apoplectic credit markets that temporarily paralyzed a broad range of financial instruments and required dramatic rescues by the U.S. Department of the Treasury and the Federal Reserve that went well beyond more traditional bank bailouts.

Looking toward the future, we also examine some relatively simple steps that mitigate and manage these operational risks. While neither complex nor prohibitively expensive, the sampling methodology, which we borrow from the auditor's toolkit and apply to loan originations, requires a substantial investment of human capital to gather sufficient loan-level information to verify asset quality.[2] Indeed, while the Basel II capital framework is making important strides in determining the amount of regulatory capital necessary for operational risk, we argue that human capital, used to assure the quality of assets underlying asset-backed securities, is an equally important form of capital that is necessary for the management of operational risk.

---

[2] The human capital investment reflects the time and energy of quality assurance and due diligence personnel who, in the case of mortgages, select the sample of mortgages, order reappraisals, verify debt, income, and credit scores, and prepare the sample summary and tests.

We proceed as follows. In section II, we present the time line of events that began in the mortgage market and rapidly brought the world's credit markets to their knees. In section III, we describe the sequence of operational failures and linkages through securitization that allowed the chain reaction to transmit trouble so broadly and so quickly. In section IV, we introduce the sampling methodology that lenders, securitizers, credit-rating agencies, investors, and regulators should have been applying to loan originations destined for the securitization network. We also describe how sampling can inhibit future operational failures and establish a quality assurance system that should dramatically limit the likelihood of another sequential and systemic failure of the sort that began in 2006. In section V, we provide brief conclusions.

II. Mortgage Mayhem

The death of Barings provides a good example of how we have come to view operational risk. An isolated incident, in the case of Barings a $1.3 billion loss attributed to unauthorized trading, proved to be catastrophic for the institution and led to bankruptcy. This billion-dollar event resulted in the demise of Barings, but it was a relatively contained crisis from the perspective of the broader financial market. Cummins, Lewis, and Wei (2006) and de Fontnouvelle, Dejesus-Rueff, Jordan, and Rosengren (2006) discuss several other relatively contained operational risk events, including losses by Daiwa Bank in 1995 and Allied Irish Banks in 2002.[3]

---

[3] Gillet, Hübner, and Plunus (2010) examine stock market returns to determine the effect of 154 operational losses at financial companies that occurred between 1990 and 2004. They find that with cases of internal fraud, stock market value fell by more than the value of the operational loss, which they interpret as evidence that the revelation of internal fraud does damage to the firm's reputation. Ritter (2008) discusses additional examples of operational risks in financial markets such as late trading in mutual funds and backdating of employee stock options. Klee (2010) looks at operational problems in sending Fedwire payments and finds that operational failures can have a measurable effect on the federal funds market.

The subprime crisis, born of operational risk, began and ended quite differently from the Barings episode. Rather than the extreme but singular incident that brought down Barings, in the recent crisis, operational risk in the mortgage industry manifested itself as multiple lapses, modest in size but pervasive in extent, that accumulated to enormous proportions and crushed many mortgage players, crippled many others, and triggered further operational crises in the adjacent mortgage-backed securities market.

What were these modest but pervasive operational failures in the mortgage industry? News reports provide an abundant supply of almost shocking revelations regarding mortgage underwriting standards across the industry that stumbled well beyond laxity into the arena of criminality.[4] Appraisal fraud, "liar loans," intimidation and retribution toward underwriters, and computer programs that steered customers into loans that were more expensive for the borrowers and more profitable for the originators, all are just pieces of the anecdotal evidence of serious problems in the mortgage industry described in these media reports.[5] But each piece of anecdotal evidence points to a realized operational risk, i.e., an operational failure.

In 2006, the first indication that underwriting problems, accompanied by rising interest rates and stalling home prices, might lead to repayment problems began to appear. Delinquencies in subprime mortgages began to increase in the third and fourth quarters of 2006. Although the overall subprime delinquency rate of 12.6 percent in the third quarter of 2006 was less than it had been as recently as the fourth quarter of 2002,

---

[4] See, for example, Streitfeld (2006), Isidore (2007), Morgenson (2007b, 2008a, 2008b, 2008c, 2008d), and Streitfeld and Morgenson (2008). An analysis by Fitch Ratings late in 2007 (see Pendley, Costello, and Kelsch (2007)) also identified widespread problems in mortgage underwriting.

[5] "Liar loans", also called stated income loans, are loans in which borrowers state their income on the loan application and the loan originator does not verify that stated income with pay stubs, W-2 forms, or some other record of income.

4

attention focused on the 13.2 percent delinquency rate among adjustable-rate subprime mortgages.[6] Concern centered on adjustable-rate mortgages (ARM) for several reasons: ARMs accounted for approximately 30 percent of all mortgage originations, and interest rates were rising, which meant more delinquencies on ARMs were likely as interest rates reset higher. The Federal Reserve had increased the federal funds rate 25 basis points to 5.25 percent on June 29, 2006, and it would keep the funds rate at that level for the remainder of 2006. The delinquency rate on adjustable-rate subprime mortgages increased to 14.4 percent in the fourth quarter of 2006. By the fourth quarter of 2007, the delinquency rate on these mortgages would increase to 20.0 percent, i.e., one delinquency for every five subprime adjustable-rate mortgages.

Weakening home prices exacerbated problems in the mortgage market. From the fourth quarter of 2005 to the first quarter of 2006, the median price of a home in the United States fell 4.1 percent.[7] With interest rates rising and home prices falling, the ingredients for making easy money in the residential real estate market disappeared, and mortgage market problems soon began to make their way into newspaper headlines.[8] Ownit Mortgage Solutions, a wholesale mortgage lender specializing in 100 percent financing of subprime mortgages, filed for bankruptcy on December 28, 2006. Mortgage Lenders Network USA Inc., another large subprime lender, went into bankruptcy on

---

[6] Delinquency data are provided by the Mortgage Bankers Association through Haver Analytics. A mortgage is delinquent if it is past due 30 days or more.

[7] The median home price is the median sales price of existing single-family homes. The data are drawn from the National Association of Realtors, accessed through Haver Analytics. The S&P/Case–Shiller Home Price Index of existing single-family homes also slowed dramatically between the fourth quarter of 2005 and the first quarter of 2006. After increasing an average of 3.0 percent per quarter from the first quarter of 2002 through the fourth quarter of 2005, the index increased only 0.9 percent during the first quarter of 2006. The quarterly change in the index turned negative in the third quarter of 2006 and remained negative until the second quarter of 2009.

[8] The appendix on pages 48–52 shows a timeline of the major events in the financial market meltdown, beginning with March 2006 and ending with January 2009.

February 5, 2007. At the beginning of March 2007, New Century Financial Corporation, the second largest subprime lender in 2006 with $51.6 billion in subprime loan originations, announced that its lenders were withdrawing the funding it relied upon for its mortgage lending operations. As a consequence, New Century announced that it was no longer accepting loan applications, and it filed for bankruptcy a month later. On August 2, 2007, American Home Mortgage Investment Corporation, the 12th-largest residential mortgage originator in 2006, also filed for bankruptcy. The first dominos, the subprime mortgage originators, had toppled.

In a Barings-like situation, the realization of losses because of operational failures in mortgage underwriting would have led to the collapse of individual mortgage originators like New Century and American Home Mortgage Investment Corporation, but the problems largely would have ended there. Unfortunately, in the crisis that was just beginning to unfold, spillovers from mortgage problems spread quickly because asset securitization and other financial market innovations, such as collateralized debt obligations (CDO) and credit default swaps (CDS), had helped place poorly underwritten subprime mortgages or their derivatives into investment portfolios around the globe. Amplifying the problem, CDOs and CDSs allowed other investors to speculate on subprime mortgage-backed securities.

Securitization is the linchpin that linked institutions and investors in a network that spread subprime problems throughout the financial system. News coverage about bankruptcy filings of subprime mortgage lenders generally identified the bankrupt companies' major creditors, and many of these creditors soon made their own way into the headlines. These creditors included such major commercial and investment banks as

Merrill Lynch, JPMorgan Chase & Co., Credit Suisse First Boston, and Countrywide Financial Corporation. Mortgage Lenders Network USA listed approximately 5,000 creditors in its bankruptcy filing. Bond houses, including Bear Stearns & Co., Lehman Brothers Holdings, Morgan Stanley, and Merrill Lynch also owned stakes in some subprime lenders to ensure a steady flow of mortgages for pooling into securities.[9] The vast securitization network that had developed around the mortgage market began to pull everyone into the subprime mortgage maelstrom that had started to churn. Operational failures in quality assurance during mortgage securitization and failures in due diligence by credit-rating agencies and investors soon amplified a mortgage market problem into a global problem and devastating financial crisis.

Because of their own operational failures in due diligence, financial institutions outside of the mortgage industry soon felt the ripple effects from the sudden collapse of the subprime mortgage market. Among the first casualties after mortgage originators were two hedge funds operated by the investment bank Bear Stearns. In July 2007, the Bear Stearns High-Grade Structured Credit Fund and the Bear Stearns High-Grade Structured Credit Enhanced Leveraged Fund filed for bankruptcy after losing essentially all of their investors' capital. But they were not alone. On August 9, 2007, BNP Paribas, a major French bank, announced that it was suspending three investment funds that invested in subprime mortgage debt. If financial markets needed further confirmation that there were serious problems in mortgages, they received it a week later when Countrywide Financial, the largest residential mortgage originator in the United States in 2006 with $455.6 billion in originations, drew down its entire $11.5 billion line of credit from a group of banks. Typically, a company draws down its credit line to increase short-

---

[9] See Reckard (2007), Keoun (2007), and Stempel (2007).

term liquidity, and Countrywide's large drawdown suggested that it had concerns about near-term liquidity or anticipated having difficulty accessing capital markets.

Late in 2007, losses from mortgage-related activities began to show up on the income statements of major commercial and investment banks. In October, Merrill Lynch announced losses of $8.4 billion, and two weeks later Citigroup announced that mortgage-related write-downs would total between $8 billion and $11 billion. The resignation of the chief executive officers of Merrill Lynch and Citigroup accompanied each of these announcements of major losses.

In early 2008, under growing pressure from mounting losses and plunging asset values, several large commercial banks and investment banks in the United States began to weaken. In January 2008, Bank of America announced that it would pay $4 billion to acquire Countrywide Financial. In March 2008, JPMorgan Chase announced that it would be acquiring most of the assets of the investment bank Bear Stearns for $2 a share, though the transaction was eventually consummated at approximately $9 a share; this was still dramatically below the 52-week high of $133 per share. In July 2008, IndyMac Bank entered into receivership with the Federal Deposit Insurance Corporation (FDIC), an event accompanied by the unnerving sight of uninsured depositors waiting in line outside the closed institution.[10]

The widening scope of the financial crisis exposed additional financial linkages, many created through securitization, and additional markets began to topple. In February 2008, responding to concerns about the soundness of monoline insurers, the International

---

[10] Although attention focused on the subprime market, losses and concerns about future losses began to undermine market confidence in almost any mortgage-backed security. Structured investment vehicles (SIV) designed to pool mortgage assets and sell debt backed by the pooled assets found that investors were refusing to buy their debt.

Swaps and Derivatives Association (ISDA) published a list of the obligations of monoline insurers.[11] Eventually this list would include over 13,000 deals with initial principal amounts of more than $1 trillion. Problems for monoline insurers began with their exposure to mortgage-backed debt guarantees, but the loss of confidence in the monoline insurers destroyed investor confidence in and hence appetite for any debt instrument guaranteed by the bond insurers. The market for auction-rate securities quickly evaporated and auction-rate security investors who thought they had bought cash-equivalent instruments found that they were holding illiquid debt. The demise of auction-rate securities almost immediately created problems for other assets, such as student loans that had been bundled into auction-rate securities. The disappearance of these supposedly cash-equivalent assets also made liquidity problems worse as investors stuck with auction-rate securities had to scramble for increasingly scarce sources of cash and liquidity.

September 2008, one of the worst months in the history of U.S. financial markets, began with the takeover of mortgage giants Fannie Mae and Freddie Mac by the U.S. government on September 7. Roughly a week later, on September 15, the investment bank Lehman Brothers declared bankruptcy. The following day, the federal government stepped in to save the insurance company American International Group (AIG) with a loan of $85 billion, and AIG's predicament exposed potentially dire problems in the massive CDS market. Among those making claims for Lehman Brothers assets were

---

[11] Monoline insurers, such as MBIA and Ambac Financial Corporation, provide financial guaranty insurance. They initially insured only municipal bonds but eventually began to insure asset-backed securities as well.

JPMorgan Chase, Credit Suisse, and GE Capital Corporation. But these large creditors were joined by smaller investors like Arapahoe County, Colorado.[12]

Losses tied to the Lehman Brothers bankruptcy also drove the net asset value of at least one money market mutual fund below a dollar, implying losses to investors in that supposedly cash-equivalent money market mutual fund. With global credit market confidence in shambles, on September 19, the Federal Reserve Board announced that it was creating a special liquidity facility to effectively support asset-backed commercial paper and money market mutual funds. By the end of September, the two surviving large investment banks Morgan Stanley and Goldman Sachs converted into bank holding companies. The FDIC seized Washington Mutual, the largest thrift institution in the United States, and the FDIC announced that Citigroup would acquire the banking assets of Wachovia Corporation—although Wells Fargo eventually purchased all of Wachovia's assets.

Dissipation of the credit markets continued into October 2008. Difficulties in the commercial paper market continued even after President Bush signed the Emergency Economic Stabilization Act of 2008 into law on October 3. On October 7, the Federal Reserve announced it was taking the extraordinary step of direct lending to the commercial paper market through the creation of a Commercial Paper Funding Facility. On October 14, using funds made available with the Emergency Economic Stabilization Act, the Treasury Department injected $250 billion in capital into major U.S. financial institutions, including Bank of America, Citibank, JPMorgan Chase, and Wells Fargo. A week later, the Federal Reserve announced the creation of the Money Market Investor Funding Facility to provide up to $540 billion to buy assets from money market mutual

---

[12] See Glater and Morgenson (2008).

funds in an effort to restore confidence in that critical market with over $3 trillion in assets.[13]

By the end of 2008, the Federal Reserve Board and the Treasury Department had implemented several more rescue operations. The Federal Reserve had lowered the Fed Funds rate below 1 percent and created the Term Asset-Backed Securities Loan Facility (TALF) to lend up to $200 billion to holders of AAA-rated securities backed by consumer and small business loans. Together, the Federal Reserve and the Treasury Department had expanded their financial support of AIG and implemented a rescue plan for Citigroup. On December 1, the National Bureau of Economic Research declared that the recession had begun in December 2007. And as if all of these financial problems were not enough, on December 13, 2008, more undetected fraud, in this case a $50 billion pyramid or "Ponzi" scheme perpetrated by investment adviser Bernard Madoff, came to light.

Table 1 shows an outline of the domino effect that began with operational failures in subprime mortgage originations and ended with the near collapse of the world's credit markets. Vertical linkages transmitted operational failures in mortgage originations all the way through the mortgage securitization process to investors. But just as important for the financial meltdown of 2007–2009 are the horizontal linkages that transmitted the shock waves from the mortgage market implosion across markets for other financial instruments and eventually throughout the world's financial system.

Contributing to the spillover problem, as the mortgage meltdown sequence showed us, operational risks within the financial system can be cumulative. Thus, as shown in table 1, credit-rating agencies and bond insurers are exposed to the operational

---

[13] Investment Company Institute, *2010 Investment Company Fact Book,* 50th edition.

risks of the mortgage originators with whom they deal, and investors are exposed to the operational risks of the entire securitization structure.[14] Research papers by Ashcraft and Schuermann (2008), Fender and Mitchell (2009), and Gotham Partners (2002) reveal how linkages form through the securitization process that transforms operational risk from an idiosyncratic problem into a systemic problem. In describing the steps taken to securitize subprime mortgages, Ashcraft and Schuermann reveal the parties that become intertwined through securitization and, because they are one and the same, the parties that each committed an operational failure that eventually allowed the chain reaction of operational failures to continue through them and engulf the world's financial markets. Similarly, in describing business and accounting problems at the monoline insurer MBIA, Gotham Partners shows us the linkages that connect insurance companies and investors to the asset-backed commercial paper market that contracted substantially in September 2008.

As Ashcraft and Schuermann describe, securitization involves many players. These players include the original borrower, the loan originator, a warehouse lender, the security issuer, the security servicer, credit-rating agencies, asset managers, and, finally, the ultimate investor.[15] Participants become exposed to operational risk anywhere within the securitization process preceding their contact with the security. Thus, the security issuer is exposed to operational risk created by the borrower or loan originator, and the investor is exposed to the operational risk of the entire securitization process.

---

[14] Table 2 repeats table 1 but populates the table with financial market participants discussed in the financial crisis timeline on pages 48–52.

[15] Whereas Ashcraft and Schuermann describe problems among the different players as information frictions, i.e., one party to a transaction with information about an asset passes along the asset to the other party but does not pass along the information about that asset, we believe that many of these frictions reflect manifestations of operational risks. For instance, some of their frictions involve mortgage fraud, predatory lending, inadequate underwriting standards, and failed due diligence by most participants.

Operational failures by participants that have already contributed to the securitization process affect any subsequent participant of that process. Although this might seem to create an overwhelming operational risk hazard for the ultimate investor in any securitized product, breaking the chain of these operational failures only requires proper due diligence with respect to the immediately preceding securitization participant, as long as that due diligence includes an operational risk report, which we describe in section IV.[16] Just as an operational failure anywhere in the securitization process can trigger cascading failures throughout the process, due diligence that effectively identifies operational failures helps to limit or eliminate subsequent spillovers.

Operational failures can spread across credit markets horizontally as well as vertically. Gotham Partners' analysis of MBIA suggests that model failures, supposedly off-balance-sheet, special-purpose vehicles (SPV) issuing commercial paper, and questionable credit ratings can lead to catastrophic problems for one firm that can paralyze entire markets. As Gotham Partners points out in its analysis, asset quality problems emerging for MBIA's SPVs likely meant that investors would not want to buy commercial paper backed by these assets. Similar problems likely contributed to the near-paralysis of the asset-backed commercial paper market in 2008 that necessitated the Federal Reserve's stepping in to guarantee most asset-backed commercial paper to prop up that market and the money market mutual funds that invest in that market.

Although the accumulation of operational risk problems is what proved to be so devastating to credit markets, the benefits from operational risk mitigation are also cumulative. Thus, proper operational risk mitigation undertaken by mortgage bundlers

---

[16] Of course, even after the mitigation of these operational risks, investors are still exposed to credit and market risks. However, the models used to manage credit and market risks should perform better with operational risks mitigated through due diligence.

helps protect the entire securitization chain. Should bundlers fail to properly address operational risk, intermediaries, such as credit-rating agencies that do undertake efforts to ensure asset quality, can still protect other market participants further down the securitization chain. In section IV, we describe our procedures for operational risk mitigation, which essentially involve quality assurance steps at the mortgage origination and bundling levels and due diligence regarding those quality assurance procedures by the other links in the securitization chain.

Before describing the risk mitigation techniques, however, in section III we suggest how operational risk afflicted financial institutions involved in the mortgage mess. Because of the massive financial rescue the crisis required, the federal government and ultimately American taxpayers bore some of the losses from these operational risks. Institutional investors, owning many "toxic" securities, had their own operational failures that led them to purchase the problematic assets, but it was their awakening to credit losses that led them to abandon many of the tainted credit markets; this action subsequently required the Federal Reserve to create special lending facilities to save these markets from complete collapse. After we show the operational risk exposure of these market players, we show the relatively simple but absolutely necessary steps securitizers must take to confront some of the unique operational risks found in structured finance.

III. Operational Risks Behind the Mortgage Mess

Subprime mortgages in and of themselves are not bad things. Properly underwritten, a subprime mortgage provides valuable access to credit for individuals and families that have blemishes on their credit histories or that have limited credit histories that result in low credit scores. Of course, being properly underwritten is the essential element necessary to make subprime lending beneficial to borrower and lender. Unfortunately, we have all witnessed the devastating consequences of poorly underwritten subprime mortgages that have ended in delinquencies and foreclosures. But what are the specific operational risks that allowed the subprime mess to happen, and how can we prevent such a disaster from happening again and restore confidence in the mortgage-backed securities market?

The financial crisis began with subprime mortgages, but the operational risks that made those subprime loans so toxic exist with any loan. Underwriting, property appraisal, and document evaluation were the problematic operational risks in subprime mortgage origination. Ironically, the presence of these operational risks was widely known by subprime market participants and their regulators, but everybody failed to notice actual problems until it was too late. As early as March 5, 1999, the federal banking agencies had issued interagency guidance on subprime lending.[17] The banking agencies defined subprime lending "as extending credit to borrowers who exhibit characteristics indicating a significantly higher risk of default than traditional bank lending customers."

Studied now, the 1999 "Interagency Guidance on Subprime Lending" reads like a prophecy from Cassandra. In providing guidance on loan purchase evaluation, the guidance warns,

> For instance, some lenders who sell subprime loans charge borrowers high up-front fees, which are usually financed into the loan. This provides incentive for originators to produce a high volume of loans with little emphasis on quality, to the detriment of a potential purchaser. Further, subprime loans, especially those purchased from outside the institution's lending area, are at special risk for fraud

---

[17] The federal banking agencies are the Board of Governors of the Federal Reserve System (Federal Reserve), the Federal Deposit Insurance Corporation, the Office of the Comptroller of the Currency (OCC), and the Office of Thrift Supervision (OTS). The document discussed here is the attachment to OCC Bulletin 1999-10, "Subprime Lending Activities," March 5, 1999 (www.occ.gov/news-issuances/bulletins/1999/bulletin-1999-10.html).

or misrepresentation (i.e., the quality of the loan may be less than the loan documents indicate).

With respect to consumer protection, the prophetic guidance continues,

> Higher fees and interest rates combined with compensation incentives can foster predatory pricing or discriminatory "steering" of borrowers to subprime products for reasons other than the borrower's underlying creditworthiness.

On model risk, loan review, and monitoring, the guidance states,

> Models driven by the volume and severity of historical losses experienced during an economic expansion may have little relevance in an economic slowdown, particularly in the subprime market.

And referring to securitization and sale hazards, the guidance foretells the coming

destruction, simply and accurately:

> Investors can quickly lose their appetite for risk in an economic downturn or when financial markets become volatile. As a result, institutions that have originated, but have not yet sold, pools of subprime loans may be forced to sell the pools at deep discounts. If an institution lacks adequate personnel, risk management procedures, or capital support to hold subprime loans originally intended for sale, these loans may strain an institution's liquidity, asset quality, earnings, and capital.

Eight years later, each of these warnings would essentially reappear in media reports but

as descriptions of the subprime meltdown rather than as warnings.[18]

Given this evidence that bankers and their regulators knew the risks of subprime

lending well and accurately, how could the subprime crisis happen?[19] Although many

factors, including rising interest rates and declining home prices contributed to the start of

the crisis, several regulatory gaps also played an important role. First, the federal banking

agencies did not regulate some of the principal participants in the subprime lending

---

[18] For the fulfillment of the perverse incentive and steering warnings, see Gretchen Morgenson (2007b). For the realization of the fraud and misrepresentation warning, see Chris Isidore (2007).

[19] Bank regulators were not the only ones aware of subprime risk; prospectuses for securities backed by subprime mortgages typically list risk factors that include less stringent underwriting standards, increased risk of loss from high loan-to-value (LTV) ratios, geographic concentrations, and the possibility that those responsible may not be able to repurchase defective mortgages.

market. Ownit Mortgage Solutions, Mortgage Lenders Network USA Inc. and New Century Financial Corporation were finance companies and not regulated by any of the federal banking agencies.[20] Though it would have been in their long-term best interests to do so, these unregulated mortgage lenders did not have to adhere to the guidance from the banking agencies and were free from the threat of enforcement actions by the agencies. Second, for the subprime participants such as IndyMac Bank and Countrywide Financial that performed poorly and were regulated by one of the banking agencies, the financial institution failed to follow guidance and the relevant banking agency failed to compel the institution to adequately comply with guidance.

While the fee structures described in the subprime guidance eliminated the originator's incentive to maintain minimal underwriting standards, regulatory shortcomings are harder to explain. Part of the problem may have been inexperience contending with operational risk in the securitization market. Before the introduction of the Basel II capital rules, regulatory capital rules for banks did not require an explicit capital charge for operational risk. Even with Basel II, the explicit capital requirement for operational risk only applies to institutions adopting the Basel II advanced approaches. As pointed out in the introduction, however, almost every bank has had experience dealing with such operational risks as mortgage fraud. Rather than inexperience with operational risk, the origins of this financial crisis had more to do with poor due diligence and shoddy underwriting that became standard practice at many institutions, especially institutions that intended to sell their mortgages.[21]

---

[20] Mortgage brokers and finance companies are generally regulated at the state level.

[21] The originate-to-sell business model also complicated regulation of subprime lending. Some mortgage originators would tend to abuse the securitization channel to hide shoddy originations. *The Big Short*:

Furthermore, for regulated banks subject to minimum regulatory capital requirements, an explicit capital charge for operational risk may not have done much good. That is because regulatory capital rules and economic capital models take a mostly passive approach to handling operational risk. Based on historical experience, the institution holds money capital in an amount sufficient to accommodate losses from a broad range of risks, including operational risk. If the current financial crisis teaches us one thing, it is that the threat from operational risks demands a much more aggressive and active response than just holding money capital. The search for and identification of a potential operational failure stemming from fraud and deceit generally require a considerable expenditure of human capital to uncover the problem.

The first step in confronting these operational risks is to identify operational risks before they become operational failures. In the case of subprime mortgages, or any mortgage, banks, bank regulatory agencies, and mortgage institutions like Fannie Mae and Freddie Mac are well aware of the steps necessary to originate a quality mortgage. Fannie Mae publishes a guide, "Originating Quality Mortgages," intended for lenders that want to sell mortgage loans to Fannie Mae. The Comptroller of the Currency includes a booklet on "Real Estate Loans (Section 213)" (www.occ.gov/static/publications /handbook /RELoans1.pdf) in the *Comptroller's Handbook* with detailed examination procedures. These guides provide a valuable blueprint for assessing the fertility of the environment for operational risks in mortgage originations. Regulated mortgage

---

Inside the Doomsday Machine by Michael Lewis (2010) provides vivid descriptions of how institutions gamed the securitization process. Cardone-Riportella, Samaniego-Medina, and Trujillo-Ponce (2010) discuss some of the motivating factors behind securitization from the perspective of Spanish banks. They identify an incentive to provide a new source of funding (enhanced liquidity) and an incentive to improve performance measures, such as return on assets and return on equity (enhanced performance), as the forces most likely to be associated with banks that elect to securitize.

originators should continue to use these guides and nonbanks must begin to apply these guidelines if they are not doing so already. But more importantly, mortgage bundlers, bond insurers, and credit-rating agencies must step into a more active quality assurance role.

Fannie Mae's *Originating Quality Mortgages* provides an adequate template for quality assurance procedures for any loan origination by any loan originator.[22] Its procedures include developing a written quality assurance plan, designating a quality assurance manager separate from the origination function, documenting results from the financial institution's quality assurance process, and conducting a review of a sample of mortgages to monitor the quality of its mortgage production. Any institution that implements and adheres to these procedures has an excellent foundation for operational risk mitigation in originating loans. Because of the vertical linkages created by securitization, however, mortgage bundlers, bond insurers, and credit-rating agencies must independently repeat the sample review portion of the quality assurance process. Potential conflicts for the quality assurance manager, regardless of whether the quality assurance process is conducted internally or outsourced, make it necessary for other links

---

[22] Fannie Mae's quality assurance guidelines include a random sample of at least 10 percent of the portfolio and a discretionary sample designed to evaluate particular mortgage brokers, employees, appraisers, or mortgage products. Fannie Mae's guide also provides a good list of what mortgage originators should cover in their mortgage reviews. This list includes validating legal and credit documentation, quality of property appraisals, and adherence to underwriting standards and regulatory requirements. While Fannie Mae's list is appropriate for the loan originator, the sampling review by bundlers, insurers, and credit-rating agencies can focus solely on validation of credit documentation and property appraisals. The stand-alone publication, *Originating Quality Mortgages*, is available at www.myclear2close.com/forms/FannieMaeQABestPractices.pdf. Fannie Mae now incorporates the quality assurance material in its publication *Selling Whole Loans to Fannie Mae*, which may be purchased at www.eFannieMae.com.

in the securitization chain to conduct a sample review as part of their due diligence of the institution preceding them in the securitization chain.[23]

IV. Operational Risk Sampling Methodology

A. Sample Design

Of course, with over 10 million mortgage applications for home purchases in 2006 and millions of mortgages making their way into mortgage-backed securities every year, it is not even remotely feasible to inspect every mortgage. Borrowing from the auditor's toolkit, however, we can draw a test sample from any portfolio and, through re-verification of several loan items, estimate the credit quality of the portfolio relative to its advertised quality. Furthermore, repeating the sampling procedure over time provides valuable information on trends in portfolio quality.

Several sampling methods are feasible for sampling asset portfolios, and the most appropriate method depends on the purpose of the inspection and who is conducting the sample inspection. Wilburn (1984) provides an excellent and thorough discussion of the various methods most appropriate for use in audit sampling. These sampling methods include random sampling, judgment sampling, discovery sampling, and flexible sampling.[24]

---

[23] Bajaj and Anderson (2008) describe how credit-rating agencies never saw details of exception reports produced by investment banks and due diligence firms that flagged high-risk loans.

[24] Besides random sampling, other sampling methods include *judgment sampling*, where an auditor or examiner uses experience and professional judgment to select a sample. This is most appropriate when the independence of the inspector is beyond question and inference to the portfolio outside of the sample is of little or no value. Thus, bank regulators may wish to use judgment sampling in examining particular aspects of a bank's operations or balance sheet. If things go poorly, however, regulators using judgment samples are always susceptible to charges of using poor judgment in deciding what to look for.

Discovery or hazard sampling is another method. With discovery sampling, which may be most appropriate when trying to find instances of fraud, the inspector defines an intolerable "critical event" and

Our objective to infer population characteristics from our sample suggests that simple random sampling is the best method with which to begin our operational risk inspection program. The first step of our inspection method, as applied to a portfolio of securitized mortgages, takes a simple random sample of the mortgages, obtains a new appraisal on each property, and verifies the borrower's income, debt, and Fair Isaac Corporation (FICO) score at the time of the loan application.[25] As part of the sample review, the sample inspector should request a review appraisal by an appraiser unaffiliated with the original appraiser, verification of income using IRS Form 4506T to request a transcript of the borrower's tax return, and a new credit report to verify the borrower's liabilities and credit score.

Although we use mortgages in describing our inspection methodology, the methodology can be applied to any asset group and should be applied to all securitized assets. Sampling and verifying property value, debt, and income allows us to calculate sample estimates for loan-to-value and debt-to-income (DTI) ratios and FICO scores. We then compare our sample estimates with the original declared values of these scores and ratios as shown in the prospectus of the mortgage-backed security.

---

sifts through the sample looking for even one instance of the critical event. If none is found, then the inspector may infer the likelihood that the universe from which the sample is drawn has less than a certain number of occurrences of the critical event. Thus, discovery sampling is useful if the inspector is looking for a single instance of a critical event for which there may be little or no tolerance. However, it may be difficult to identify an appropriate threshold to define the critical event, and, once there is a particular threshold, dishonest participants may quickly adapt to operating just under the threshold. Because of this gaming threat, discovery sampling may be most appropriate for irregular or nonsystematic spot checks.

Flexible sampling, which integrates examiner judgment and prior knowledge with statistical features, seeks to identify material problems. Flexible sampling may be the most appropriate method for auditors to use. However, because of the potential problems we identified with judgment and discovery sampling, flexible sampling may not be the best sampling method to use when the purpose of the inspection is to assess the reliability of credit quality factors in a large portfolio, which is the principal aim of our operational risk inspection.

[25] The tolerance level for critical differences in appraisals will want to take into consideration reasonable fluctuations in property values that occur over time.

Each entity issuing an asset-backed security must file a prospectus with the U.S. Securities and Exchange Commission (SEC). The prospectus provides potential investors and credit-rating agencies with information on the asset pool backing the security. The prospectus includes information on the principal balances of the loans, the number of loans in the pool, average interest rates, loan-to-value ratios, FICO credit scores, and interest rate caps— to name a few of the reported data items. The prospectus provides data in the aggregate and for a large number of different categories, such as fixed-rate loans, adjustable-rate loans, credit scores, and property types. A prospectus, which typically can be as long as 300 pages for a single security, contains an impressive amount of data regarding the asset pool. Regrettably, all of this prospectus information is unverified, and this proved to be the Achilles' heel of the securitization channel, where operational risk took up residence and, in the future, where inspection sampling can do the most good.

Three items in the prospectus are of interest from an operational risk sampling perspective. As we saw in section III, the mortgage meltdown resulted from, to put it bluntly, originators cramming garbage into the securitization conduit—the operational risks that apply to loan originations most often affected appraisal values, overstated income, and understated debt. Thus, we are interested in the following reported values from the prospectus: the weighted-average original LTV ratio, the weighted-average debt-to-income ratio, and, to a lesser extent, the weighted-average original FICO score.

Independent verification of property value and the borrower's income and liabilities for a random sample allow us to construct unbiased estimates of the mean LTV ratio and the mean DTI ratio for the entire pool of mortgages. We can then compare these unbiased estimates with the known population values for each ratio to determine an estimate of the LTV and DTI errors for the mortgage pool as a whole. The estimated LTV and DTI ratios in turn may convey information regarding default probabilities and loss given default.[26] It is also feasible to use an indicator variable to identify the presence of an error above some specified percentage, but as our objective is to assess the accuracy of values reported in the prospectus, we focus on verifying the specific value of our variables of interest.

In gathering the information on the sample of mortgages, we could also develop estimates for the mean appraisal error, income error, and liabilities error in the mortgage pool. By tracking information on appraisers and originators across different mortgage pools, we can use these error estimates to grade individual appraisers and originators. This may be of help later if an inspection suggests that sample stratification and discovery sampling may be informative, but we defer this topic to future research.

We now demonstrate our sampling methodology using a mortgage-backed security. Table 3 presents data on the mortgages underlying a mortgage-backed security issued by Goldman Sachs in 2006, GSAMP 2006-NC2.[27] The aggregate pool of mortgages for this security is our universe. Column A of table 3 shows the reported universe value for several variables taken from the prospectus. Columns B through D list estimates for these variables based on samples of 50, 100, and 200 mortgages, respectively.

---

[26] See Qi and Yang (2009) for a discussion of the impact of LTV ratios for residential mortgages on loss given default.

[27] This is the security discussed in Ashcraft and Schuermann (2008). LoanPerformance, now a part of CoreLogic, provides loan-level data on mortgage-backed securities, including loan-level data on GSAMP 2006-NC2.

With the *t*-statistic that we use later to compare sample means with reported means, we show how the tolerance limit for deviations from the reported means falls as sample size increases. Figure 1 shows, for a significance level of 0.05, that the tolerance limit for deviations from the reported LTV drops quickly, from over 7 with a sample size of 10 to just over 2 with a sample size of 100 and just under 2 with a sample size of 200. In other words, if the sample size is 10, then the sample LTV would have to be nearly 8 percentage points higher than the reported LTV before the test could reject the null hypothesis that the sample LTV and the reported LTV are equal. If the sample size is 100, then LTV deviations of roughly 2.4 percentage points lead to rejection of the null hypothesis. Although, as table 3 and figure 1 show, a random sample of as few as 50 mortgages provides both a reasonable approximation to the universe and a reasonable trade-off between tolerance limits and sample size, we elect to use 100 mortgages randomly selected for our inspection. The *p* values shown in table 3 inform us that our sample means do not, in any of the samples, differ significantly from the reported universe mean.

If we were performing the actual inspection, we would draw a random sample of 100 mortgages from the pool and request new appraisals and verifications of borrower debt and income as discussed at the beginning of this section. Unfortunately, we can only simulate an inspection and report the results of the simulation. Using LoanPerformance data on the underlying mortgages, we are able to explore how differences in appraisal values would affect reported LTV ratios. Again, in the simulation we have to be content with this single variable, as the LoanPerformance data do not report the underlying information on debt and income. We could manipulate the DTI ratio as we do the appraisal value, but because the methodology and effects would be the same, we limit our discussion to the results pertaining to LTV ratios.

When looking at a specific security, we randomly select 100 mortgages from all loans underlying that security. After verifying the appraisal value, borrower debt, and borrower income, we are able to calculate sample means and confidence intervals for our LTV and DTI ratios. We can also calculate weighted sample means and corresponding confidence intervals to match the weighted-average information disclosed in the prospectus. For example, we compute the weighted sample mean for the LTV ratio as

$$\hat{\bar{y}} = \frac{\sum_{i=1}^{n} w_i y_i}{\sum_{i=1}^{n} w_i} \qquad (1)$$

where y_i is the LTV ratio for mortgage i, w_i is the weight for mortgage i calculated as the closing balance of mortgage i, and n is the size of the sample. We then calculate the confidence limits for the mean as

$$\hat{\bar{y}} \pm StdErr(\hat{\bar{y}}) * t_{df,\alpha/2} \qquad (2)$$

where $StdErr$ is the standard error of the sample estimate of the mean, and $t_{df,\alpha/2}$ is the t-statistic for degrees of freedom, df, and confidence coefficient α. We then use a t-test to compare the sample means with the means reported in the prospectus,

$$t = \frac{\hat{\bar{y}} - \mu}{s/\sqrt{n}} \qquad (3)$$

where μ is the mean reported in the prospectus, s is the sample standard deviation, and n is the sample size.

Dissecting equation 3 shows how sampling and the t-test allow us to identify systematic bias in a pool of mortgages. In the numerator, if the new appraisals underlying the sample LTV are consistently lower than the original appraisals, then the sample LTV ($\hat{\bar{y}}$) tends to be greater than the reported LTV (μ) and the numerator increases. In the denominator, the t-test uses the sample standard deviation, which measures deviations from the sample mean rather than deviations from the reported mean. Large deviations within the sample increase s, making the t-statistic smaller and making it less likely to reject the null hypothesis that the means are equal. Thus, results that reject the null hypothesis provide strong evidence that there is systematic bias in the pool.[28]

Each of our three variables of interest—the LTV ratio, FICO scores, and the debt-to-income ratio—are subject to some uncertainty. For instance, the very nature of appraisals, estimating the value of a home based on comparable but not identical home sales, introduces uncertainty into LTV ratios. Uncertainty, however, is not bias. Uncertainty suggests that appraisal errors, or honest differences in appraised values, are relatively evenly distributed around zero. Thus, it would not be surprising to find new appraisals that are 5 percent or even 10 percent above or below the original appraisal. Such general uncertainty associated with each of our variables tends to have offsetting effects in our sample and would not necessarily lead us to reject the null hypothesis of equal means. Our t-test can accommodate the general uncertainty associated with our variables of interest while identifying the presence of systematic bias.

Figure 2 demonstrates how bias in a variable of interest affects the mean as the error rate increases. Figure 2 shows the hypothetical situation in which all loans in a pool have equal weight and equal LTVs of 80 percent. Each line in figure 2 traces the new

---

[28] For example, in the extreme case when all new appraisals in the sample result in a new LTV that is some constant c points higher than the original, then the sample mean and the numerator in the t-test will be c points higher, but the standard deviation and the denominator will not change. This merely reflects the fact that the addition of a constant will increase the sample mean by that constant but will not change the sample variance or standard deviation.

LTV ratio for a given appraisal error as the share of the population with the error increases. Thus, following the line for a 5 percent appraisal error, if each new appraisal reports a value that is 5 percent lower, the new LTV slowly rises from the reported value of 80 percent to approximately 84 percent. Similarly, with a 20 percent appraisal error, the new LTV rises more quickly as it approaches 100 percent if all the new appraisals are 20 percent lower than the original appraisals.

To illustrate how our sampling methodology would work, we demonstrate by randomly drawing a sample of 100 mortgages from the pool, GSAMP 2006-NC2. As mentioned before, in an actual inspection, we would then calculate the sample means and confidence limits after verifying, in this case, appraisal values. In our simulations, however, we have to be content with manipulating the data artificially and then investigating how effective sampling is at detecting the change. To show how poor asset quality can affect the sample estimates in our simulation, we first randomly "infect" part of our universe with fixed appraisal errors: we assign a new appraisal that is less than the original appraisal. We illustrate the effect of overstated collateral values by gradually increasing the appraisal error and the share of the population we infect with the simulated error. Thus, we randomly infect 10 percent of our population with a 10 percent error rate, then 20 percent of our population with a 20 percent error rate, 30 percent of our population with a 30 percent error rate, and 50 percent of our population with a 50 percent error rate. After infecting our population, we then draw a new random sample of 100 mortgages and estimate our sample means and confidence limits. Table 4 reports the results from our simulations.

The results shown in table 4 have two implications. First, as the infection and error rates increase, the 95 percent confidence interval for the LTV ratio gradually moves away from the universe mean of 78.60 percent.[29] At a 20 percent infection rate with 20 percent error severity, the confidence interval no longer includes the reported mean and a t-test with a 95 percent confidence level rejects the hypothesis that the sample mean is equal to the reported value of the mean, as shown in table 5. Second, the sample mean continues to closely track the true mean of the infected population, and t-tests do not reject the hypothesis that the two values are equal. Table 4 also shows that the number of errors found in the sample is relatively consistent with the population infection rate.[30]

The information in table 4 indicates the potential power of asset inspection using a simple random sample of 100 mortgages. Applied here to a mortgage-backed security, this method is applicable to any asset-backed security. Clearly, a sample LTV ratio that differs significantly from the reported LTV ratio should raise red flags for bundlers, credit-rating agencies, investors, and regulatory agencies.

From the perspective of mitigating operational risk, it is important that sampling occur before issuing a security. Sampling, however, can also provide information on the health of a security after issuance. Using information on actual losses incurred with GSAMP 2006-NC2 as reported by LoanPerformance with its January 2009 data, we can

---

[29] The mean of the combined LTV reported in the prospectus and shown in table 3 is 80.34 percent. To run our simulations, we calculated our own LTV as the ratio of the closing balance to the appraisal value reported in the LoanPerformance data. The weighted average of our calculated LTV is 78.60 percent for the population universe, which we use as the "reported" value for our mean comparisons.

[30] We also conducted simulations holding the universe infection rate at 10 percent while increasing the severity of the appraisal error and simulations holding the severity of the appraisal error at 10 percent while increasing the universe infection rate. The sampling inspection seems to be slightly more sensitive to universe infection rates than error severity. Holding the error severity constant at 10 percent, the 95 percent confidence interval excluded the reported mean when 30 percent of the universe became infected. The error severity had to be 50 percent for the confidence interval to exclude the reported mean when the infection rate was fixed at 10 percent.

construct an ex post LTV ratio as the ratio of the original loan balance to the difference between the original appraisal and the amount of the loss. If there is no loss, then this ex post LTV is equal to the reported LTV. The January 2009 LTV for our sample of 100 mortgages is 93.68 percent with a 95 percent confidence interval between 82.24 percent and 105.11 percent, well above the reported LTV of 78.60. These results reflect the weakness in GSAMP 2006-NC2 that had already occurred by January 2009 as a consequence of multiple factors, including the deterioration of the housing market.

B. Reporting Inspection Results

Reporting the results of the inspection is just as important as the actual sampling and verification of the underlying assets. Because of vertical and horizontal linkages, information from the sampling report strengthens the entire financial market. Individual investors and investment managers may have the most to gain from operational risk reporting, because they are the participants that ultimately purchase a potentially toxic security. Sampling allows the disclosure of operational risk reports for the lender, third-party originators, mortgage brokers, and correspondents.

Table 6 shows a template for an operational risk inspection report. Table 7 populates the template using information from one of our simulation samples. Several fields in the template include information from the prospectus about the portfolio. The portfolio description section should list basic identifying information about the portfolio. The reports should also include reported values related to the inspection variables along with the source for those values, which in our case is the prospectus.

The inspector then populates the remaining fields based on the sample results. In addition to identifying the specific variables that the inspection is verifying for the sample, the inspector should define critical events for each of those inspection variables. For instance, it is highly likely that the original appraisal and the verified appraisal will differ by thousands of dollars. Thus, it is more appropriate to define a critical event, or serious error, as something more substantial. Inspector experience and knowledge help to define critical events, which should be consistent across similar portfolios. The definitions for critical events themselves provide information to potential investors, giving them a sense of the precision that typically accompanies a particular portfolio. Note that critical events are one-sided, reflecting their role as risk indicators. Verified income that is substantially higher than reported income is not likely to increase the risk of the portfolio, for example.

For each of the inspection variables, the report should indicate the number of critical events found in the verified sample and information regarding the overall (critical and noncritical) differences between reported and verified values. The minimum and maximum values along with the mean give an indication of the extent to which the errors are distributed around zero. For instance, in our simulation, we only reduced the value of property relative to the original appraisal. This results in a minimum appraisal difference of zero, which means that all appraisal errors overstated the value of the property. Such a problem would most likely be a cause for great concern among potential investors.

Finally, the inspection report then presents the derived variables for the sample. After verifying the appraisal value, the inspector constructs a new weighted-average sample mean, determines the 95 percent confidence interval, and tests whether the sample mean is significantly different from the reported value. We also include the sample median because a comparison of the mean and the median suggest the degree and direction of skewness in the sample. The completed inspection report should then become part of the portfolio, accompanying the prospectus for perusal by potential investors.

C. Who Should Conduct Operational Risk Inspections?

Although any institution that is contemplating investing in a portfolio of loans should be inclined to conduct inspections as described in this section, we believe that the maximum universal benefit from the inspections ensues if nationally recognized statistical rating organizations (NRSRO) incorporate such inspections into their rating process and the SEC mandates and supervises the sampling procedure as part of its supervision of NRSROs. Regulated banks and loan originators securitizing through Fannie Mae and Freddie Mac should already sample their mortgages and other loans as part of the regulatory examination process or quality assurance process. To our knowledge, however, these examinations do not produce the type of risk report we advocate. Thus, regulated banks and bank regulators may wish to incorporate inspections and reports similar to those described in section IV into their examination procedures. These reports would be of great value to any institution's chief risk officer.

Investors owning securitized assets and those that securitize assets stand to gain considerably from our sample inspection reports, but it is not feasible for them to conduct the inspections themselves because of data access and conflict-of-interest issues, respectively. Thus, it falls to the rating agencies and monoline insurers to conduct these inspections because of their ability to get access to underlying loan-level information on the securities they rate or insure, respectively. Furthermore, we do not see how a rating agency can accurately rate any asset-backed security without verifying the accuracy of loan-level data.

31

The fundamental weakness in how rating agencies rate asset-backed securities is one of the problems exposed by the subprime loan financial crisis. This fundamental weakness is the reliance on historical data regarding comparable assets. The rating process can continue to use historical data to estimate transition and default probabilities, but it must conduct inspections as we describe in order to verify that the current vintage of assets is indeed comparable to the historical vintages. To appreciate the critical importance of this simple verification step, just consider the damage that might have been avoided if the rating agencies had tested the comparability of subprime mortgage securities issued in 2003 against those issued in 2006.[31]

Although bankers and bank examiners inspect samples of mortgages as part of their internal or regulatory examination procedures, they may wish to adopt the sampling inspection methodology with data verification and reporting as described in section IV above to complement the implementation of operational risk efforts being introduced in conjunction with Basel II regulatory capital requirements.[32] The sample inspection report shown in tables 6 and 7 should serve as a useful tool for chief risk officers, senior bank management, bank directors, and bank regulators.

Sample inspections conducted by credit-rating agencies would also extend critical oversight to nonbanks that seek access to global credit markets through the securitization channel. Any nonbank seeking to securitize assets it originates would have to pass the

---

[31] Fitch Ratings (Pendley, Costello, and Kelsch (2007)) conducted an analysis of poorly performing mortgage-backed securities. The analysis included a file review of 45 mortgages with early missed payments that revealed "the appearance of fraud or misrepresentation in almost every file." Despite these findings, surprisingly Fitch dismisses a data reverification role for itself and prefers to address the problems by assessing underwriting processes and controls during originator reviews.

[32] See Davis (2005) for a thorough presentation of many of the methods large regulated banking organizations are starting to use as part of the implementation of Basel II's Advance Measurement Approaches to operational risk management.

rating agencies' inspection verifying comparable asset quality. To appreciate the importance of this step, recall the story of New Century at the start of the financial crisis. If the rating agencies had detected the toxicity of New Century's mortgages sooner and limited its access to the securitization channel, New Century's operational failures in underwriting would probably have left us with a story similar to the Barings debacle rather than the cascading failures that came in the wake of New Century's collapse. New Century's failures would have cost them dearly and they likely would have ended in failure. Like Barings, however, it would have been another operational risk tragedy with terrible consequences for those responsible but with consequences limited to those responsible.[33]

V. Conclusion

In this study, we describe the economic crisis that began in the U.S. subprime mortgage market in late 2006 as a consequence of cascading operational failures. Old operational risks, such as mortgage fraud and lack of due diligence, combined with modern financial players, such as nonbanks and financial engineers assembling asset-backed securities, to initiate a nearly catastrophic crisis in financial markets and a painful recession that is the longest on record since the Great Depression.[34] Operational failures in the credit-rating process by credit-rating agencies and monoline insurers and

---

[33] Fender and Mitchell (2009) suggest that requiring a retained interest in a securitization could help restore responsibility to and confidence in the securitization market. However, they point out that some sophisticated financial institutions suffered substantial losses on AAA-rated tranches that the institutions themselves had originated. They conclude that retained interests may not align incentives for all securitization transactions, especially if an economic downturn is likely.

[34] The National Bureau of Economic Research dates business cycles in the United States. According to the bureau, before the current crisis, the longest contractions after the Great Depression lasted 16 months, from November 1973 to March 1975 and from July 1981 to November 1982. In September 2010, the bureau announced that the recession trough had occurred in June 2009, terminating the "Great Recession" at 18 months.

operational failures in due diligence by investors allowed toxic assets to permeate throughout global credit markets. When the first domino fell in the subprime market, it exposed these other operational failures along with their accompanying losses in a terrifying chain-reaction that radiated along vertical and horizontal market linkages until it had utterly destroyed confidence in the world's credit markets. Only dramatic and blanket guarantees by the Treasury Department, the Federal Reserve, and the FDIC saved the world's credit markets from almost complete paralysis.

To avoid a repetition of such a crisis born of operational risk and to help restore confidence in the securitization market, we propose an asset inspection methodology that employs simple random sampling and direct verification of loan-level information. We describe how this sampling and confirmation procedure can verify critical asset quality information reported in a security's prospectus and demonstrate this procedure with a simulation exercise applied to a mortgage-backed security, GSAMP 2006-NC2. We provide a template for reporting the results from the sampling inspection. The inspection report must then become part of the security's prospectus. The information in this inspection report is of great use to investors, loan originators, and bank regulators, but it is of essential importance for credit-rating agencies and monoline insurers. The credit-rating agencies should incorporate the inspection report into their rating process as a means of verifying that the security they are rating is comparable in quality to the securities they are using to model historical default risk.

It is vital that the credit-rating agencies, or their proxies, become involved in sampling inspections, because failures by the credit-rating agencies expose the entire securitization market to a potential crisis of confidence. Investors rely heavily on the credit-rating agencies for an assessment of the riskiness of a particular asset. Widespread

mistakes in credit ratings strike a blow to the credibility of the rating agencies and lead

reasonable investors to question the validity of any credit rating. In such a scenario,

investors would likely abandon most rated securities and flock to U.S. government

securities, which, of course, is exactly what happened in 2008. So critical is the need for

sampling of structured finance products at the pivotal credit-rating stage that should the

credit-rating agencies fail to adopt such a methodology voluntarily, the SEC should make

it a condition for granting NRSRO designation for an agency rating structured-finance

products.[35]

It almost certainly did not help confidence in the financial markets that the two

Bear Stearns hedge funds that imploded in June 2007 included "high-grade" in the fund's

name. In addition to raising the possibility that other "high-grade" investments might not

be so high grade after all, the failure of the Bear Stearns funds exposed other concerns;

namely, the speed with which the funds collapsed, that Bear Stearns was a major player

in the mortgage securities market, and the obvious failure or absence of effective risk

management.[36] These concerns would certainly rattle any risk-sensitive institutional

investor. They may have contributed to problems in the auction-rate securities market,

which began slowing in August 2007 and stopped completely in February 2008. Similar

risk assessment failures could also allow insurance companies, such as AIG, to write

---

[35] Stolper (2009) presents a model of credit-rating agency regulation that suggests that regulators can alter credit-rating agency behavior by reducing the future number of approved credit-rating agencies based on relative rating performance.

[36] See Morgenson, (2007a).

$656 billion in credit insurance on structured finance products with only $54 billion in resources to pay those claims.[37]

The sampling methodology exposes liar loans and mortgage fraud, and it effectively applies quality assurance supervision to nonbanks seeking access to the securitization channel. In addition to providing a current assessment of the quality of assets underlying an asset-backed security, the sampling inspection report should help restore confidence in the securitization market. Restoring confidence in these securities is necessary to allow for the eventual withdrawal of the Federal Reserve's guarantees issued through the TALF that is currently helping to prop up the asset-backed securities market.

In subsequent research, we will describe how credit-rating agencies and loan originators can use information from inspection sampling to grade various participants in the loan origination process. In the case of the mortgage market, these participants would include the property appraisers and loan originators. Even without grading participants, the basic version of the sampling inspection should quickly and dramatically increase the quality of securitized assets and the reliability of pool data reported in asset-backed security prospectuses.

---

[37] See Morgenson (2008d).

References

Ashcraft, Adam B., and Til Schuermann. 2008. "Understanding the Securitization of Subprime Mortgage Credit," Federal Reserve Bank of New York, Staff Report 318.

Bajaj, Vikas, and Jenny Anderson. 2008. "Inquiry Focuses on Withholding of Data on Loans," *The New York Times*, January 12.

Basel Committee on Banking Supervision. 2006. *Basel II: International Convergence of Capital Measurement and Capital Standards: A Revised Framework—Comprehensive Version.* Bank for International Settlements, June.

Cardone-Riportella, Clara, Reyes Samaniego-Medina, and Antonio Trujillo-Ponce. 2010. "What Drives Bank Securitisation? The Spanish Experience," *Journal of Banking & Finance,* Vol. 34(11), pp. 2639–2651.

Cummins, J. David, Christopher M. Lewis, and Ran Wei. 2006. "The Market Value Impact of Operational Loss Events for US Banks and Insurers," *Journal of Banking & Finance,* Vol. 30(10), pp. 2605–2634.

Davis, Ellen, ed. 2005. *Operational Risk: Practical Approaches to Implementation.* London: Risk Books.

De Fontnouvelle, Patrick, Virginia Dejesus-Rueff, John S. Jordan, and Eric S. Rosengren. 2006. "Capital and Risk: New Evidence on Implications of Large Operational Losses," *Journal of Money, Credit, and Banking,* Vol. 38(7), pp. 1819–1846.

Engen, John. 2008. "Future Shock," *U.S. Banker,* Vol. 118(9), pp. 24–29.

Fender, Ingo, and Janet Mitchell. 2009. "The Future of Securitisation: How to Align Incentives?" *Bank for International Settlements Quarterly Review,* September, pp. 27–43.

Gillet, Roland, Georges Hübner, and Séverine Plunus. 2010. "Operational Risk and Reputation in the Financial Industry," *Journal of Banking & Finance,* Vol. 34(1), pp. 224–235.

Glater, Jonathan D., and Gretchen Morgenson. 2008. "A Fight for a Piece of What's Left," *The New York Times*, September 16.

Gotham Partners Management Co. 2002. "Is MBIA Triple A?" manuscript, December 9.

Isidore, Chris. 2007. " 'Liar Loans': Mortgage Woes Beyond Subprime," CNNMoney.com, March 19.

Keoun, Bradley. 2007. "Ownit Files for Bankruptcy as Merrill Seeks to Return Bad Loans," www.Bloomberg.com, January 2.

Klee, Elizabeth. 2010. "Operational Outages and Aggregate Uncertainty in the Federal Funds Market," *Journal of Banking & Finance,* Vol. 34(10), pp. 2386–2402.

Lewis, Michael. 2010. *The Big Short: Inside the Doomsday Machine.* New York. W.W. Norton.

Morgenson, Gretchen. 2007a. "Fair Game; When Models Misbehave," *The New York Times*, June 24.

Morgenson, Gretchen. 2007b. "Inside the Countrywide Lending Spree," *The New York Times*, August 26.

Morgenson, Gretchen. 2008a. "Lender Tells Judge It 'Recreated' Letters," *The New York Times*, January 8.

Morgenson, Gretchen. 2008b. "Lenders Who Sold and Left," *The New York Times*, February 3.

Morgenson, Gretchen. 2008c. "A Road Not Taken by Lenders," *The New York Times*, April 6.

Morgenson, Gretchen. 2008d. "Naked Came the Speculators," *The New York Times,* August 10.

Morgenson, Gretchen. 2008e. "Was There a Loan It Didn't Like?" *The New York Times*, November 2.

Pendley, M. Diane, Glenn Costello, and Mary Kelsch. 2007. "The Impact of Poor Underwriting Practices and Fraud in Subprime RMBS Performance," *U.S. Residential Mortgage Special Report,* www.fitchratings.com, November 28.

Qi, M., and X. Yang. 2009. "Loss Given Default of High Loan-to-Value Residential Mortgages," *Journal of Banking & Finance,* Vol. 33(5), pp. 788–799.

Reckard, E. Scott. 2007. "Demise of Ownit Mortgage Hits Home," *Los Angeles Times,* January 3.

Ritter, Jay R. 2008. "Forensic Finance," *Journal of Economic Perspectives,* Vol. 22 (Summer), pp. 127-147.

Stempel, Jonathan. 2007. "Mortgage Lenders Network USA Files for Chapter 11," www.reuters.com, February 5.

Stolper, Anno. 2009. "Regulation of Credit Rating Agencies," *Journal of Banking & Finance*, Vol. 33(7), pp. 1266–1273.

Streitfeld, David. 2006. "More Home Buyers Stretch Truth, Budgets to Get Loans," *Los Angeles Times*, September 29.

Streitfeld, David, and Gretchen Morgenson. 2008. "Building Flawed American Dreams," *The New York Times*, October 19.

Wilburn, Arthur J. 1984. *Practical Statistical Sampling for Auditors,* New York: Marcel Dekker.

Tables and Figures

Table 1. Operational Risk Linkages in the Mortgage Market

Institution	Operational Risks	Vertical Linkages	Horizontal Linkages
A. Mortgage Originator	Underwriting, Property Appraisal, Document Evaluation	Mortgage Bundler	Other Loan Originations
B. Mortgage Bundler	Due Diligence of Mortgage Originators	Bond Insurers and Credit-Rating Agencies	Other Bundles
C. Bond Insurers and Credit-Rating Agencies	Due Diligence of Mortgage Originators and Mortgage Bundlers	Investment Managers	Other Bonds and Other Rated Securities
D. Investment Managers	Due Diligence of Mortgage Originators, Mortgage Bundlers, Bond Insurers, and Credit-Rating Agencies	Investors	Other Investments
E. Investors	Due Diligence of Mortgage Originators, Mortgage Bundlers, Bond Insurers, Credit-Rating Agencies, and Investment Managers	Creditors	Other Credits

Table 2. Populated Operational Risk Linkages in the Mortgage Market

Institution	Operational Risks	Vertical Linkages	Horizontal Linkages
A. Mortgage Originators: New Century, IndyMac	Underwriting, Property Appraisal, Document Evaluation	Fannie Mae, Bear Stearns, Goldman Sachs, JPMorgan Chase	Other Loan Originations
B. Mortgage Bundlers: Fannie Mae, Bear Stearns, Goldman Sachs, Merrill Lynch, JPMorgan Chase, Cheyne Capital Management	Due Diligence of New Century, IndyMac	Ambac, MBIA, S&P, Moody's	SIVs, Auction-Rate Securities, Asset-Backed Commercial Paper
C. Bond Insurers and Credit-Rating Agencies: Ambac, MBIA, S&P, Moody's, Fitch	Due Diligence of New Century, IndyMac, Fannie Mae, Bear Stearns, Goldman Sachs, Merrill Lynch, JPMorgan Chase, Cheyne Capital Management	Investment Managers	Auction-Rate Securities, Mortgage-Backed Securities, Asset-Backed Securities, Other Rated Securities, CDOs, CDSs
D. Investment Managers	Due Diligence of New Century, IndyMac, Fannie Mae, Bear Stearns, Goldman Sachs, Merrill Lynch, JPMorgan Chase, Cheyne Capital Management, Ambac, MBIA, S&P, Moody's, Fitch	Investors	Other Investments
E. Investors	Due Diligence of New Century, IndyMac, Fannie Mae, Bear Stearns, Goldman Sachs, Merrill Lynch, JPMorgan Chase, Cheyne Capital Management, Ambac, MBIA, S&P, Moody's, Fitch, and Investment Managers	Creditors	Other Credits

Table 3. Universe and Sample Data for GSAMP 2006-NC2 *(p Values in Parentheses for Comparison of Sample and Universe Means)*

Variable	(A) Universe (Prospectus)	(B) Sample Size 50	(C) Sample Size 100	(D) Sample Size 200
Total Principal Balance	$881,499,701	$9,730,857	$20,278,243	$42,519,321
Number of Mortgages	3,949	50	100	200
Weighted-Average (WA) Original FICO	626	631.8 (0.3792)	626.5 (0.9306)	625.1 (0.8176)
WA Combined LTV with Silent Seconds	80.34%	81.01% (0.5115)	80.27% (0.9274)	81.25% (0.1937)
WA DTI Ratio at Origination	41.78%	40.30% (0.1812)	41.15% (0.4488)	41.15% (0.3420)

Table 4. LTV Ratio Simulation Sample Means and Confidence Limits, GSAMP 2006-NC2 (3,949 Mortgages)

Sample	*n*	Percent Infected (number infected)	Appraisal Error Rate	Errors Found	True Mean	Sample Mean	Lower 95% Limit	Upper 95% Limit
Universe	3,949	0	0	NA	78.60	NA	NA	NA
1	100	0	0	NA	78.60	78.29	76.48	80.10
2	100	10% (395)	10%	7	79.45	79.04	77.20	80.89
3	100	20% (790)	20%	16	82.33	81.54	79.12	83.96
4	100	30% (1185)	30%	31	88.59	89.20	85.01	93.39
5	100	50% (1875)	50%	46	115.75	114.46	104.99	123.94

Table 5. *t*-Tests, LTV Ratio Simulation Sample Means, and Reported Mean, GSAMP 2006-NC2 (3,949 Mortgages)

Sample	*n*	Percent Infected	Appraisal Error Rate	Sample Mean	*p* Value, Sample Mean Equals Reported Mean
Universe	3,949	0	0	78.60	NA
1	100	0	0	78.29	0.7583
2	100	10%	10%	79.04	0.6660
3	100	20%	20%	81.54	0.0219
4	100	30%	30%	89.20	< 0.0001
5	100	50%	50%	114.46	< 0.0001

Table 6. Sample Inspection Report Example

Sample Inspection Report					
Portfolio Description					
Definition of Critical Events					
Reported Values (Source)					
WA LTV					
WA DTI					
WA FICO					
Sample Values (Sample Size = n)					
Inspection Variables					
Variable	Critical Events Found	Reported—Verified Mean	Reported—Verified Minimum	Reported—Verified Maximum	Reported—Verified Range
Property Appraisal					
Borrower Income					
Borrower Debt					
Borrower FICO					
Derived Values					
Variable	Sample Median	Sample Mean	Lower 95% Confidence Limit	Upper 95% Confidence Limit	p Value, Sample Mean Equals Reported Mean
WA LTV					
WA DTI					
WA FICO					

44

Table 7. Sample Inspection Report, Simulation Exercise With 20 Percent Error Infection and Severity Rates

Sample Inspection Report					
Portfolio Description	GSAMP 2006-NC2, a pool of 3,949 first- and second-lien 1-to-4-family home mortgages with a total principal balance of $881,499,701				
Definition of Critical Events	1. Verified Appraisal Value < 0.85 * Reported Appraisal Value 2. Verified Income < 0.85 * Reported Income 3. Verified Debt > 1.15 * Reported Debt 4. Verified FICO < 0.85 * Reported FICO				
Reported Values (Source: Prospectus)					
WA LTV	80.34%				
WA DTI	41.78%				
WA FICO	626				
Sample Values (Sample Size = 100)					
Inspection Variables					
Variable	Critical Events Found	Reported—Verified Mean	Reported—Verified Minimum	Reported—Verified Maximum	Reported—Verified Range
Property Appraisal	16	$13,031	$0	$182,000	$182,000
Borrower Income	NA	NA	NA	NA	NA
Borrower Debt	NA	NA	NA	NA	NA
Borrower FICO	NA	NA	NA	NA	NA
Derived Values					
Variable	Sample Median	Sample Mean	Lower 95% Confidence Limit	Upper 95% Confidence Limit	p Value, Sample Mean Equals Reported Mean
WA LTV	79.96%	81.54%	79.12%	83.96%	0.0219
WA DTI	NA	NA	NA	NA	NA
WA FICO	NA	NA	NA	NA	NA

Figure 1. Tolerance Limit to LTV Deviation as Sample Size Increases, alpha=.05

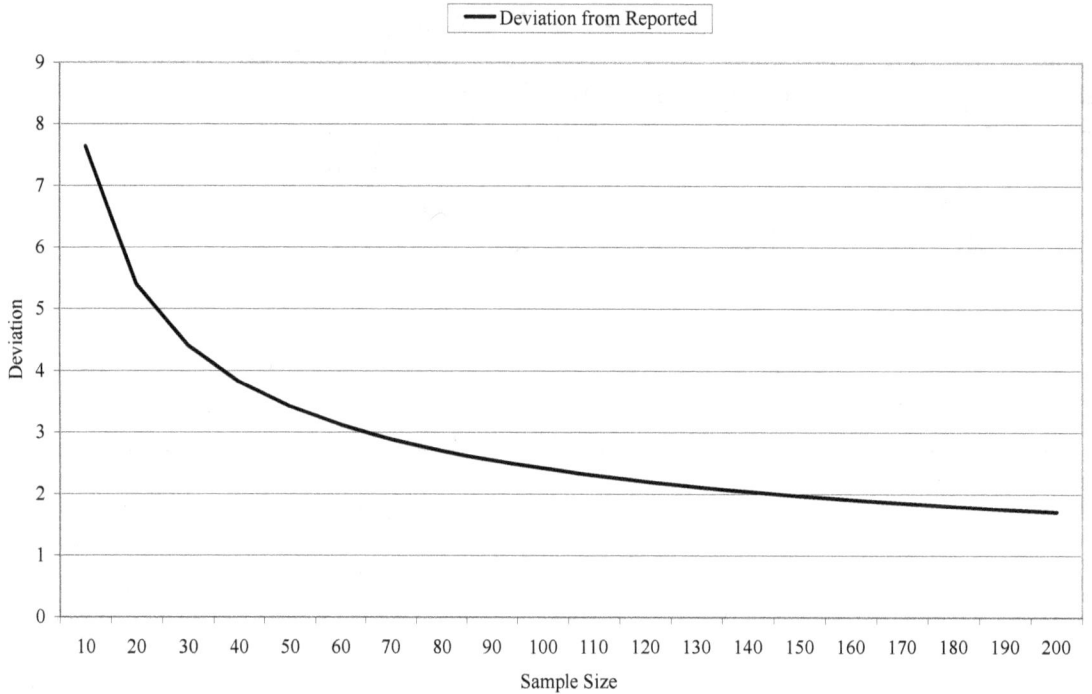

Figure 2. Effect of Appraisal Errors on LTV Ratio

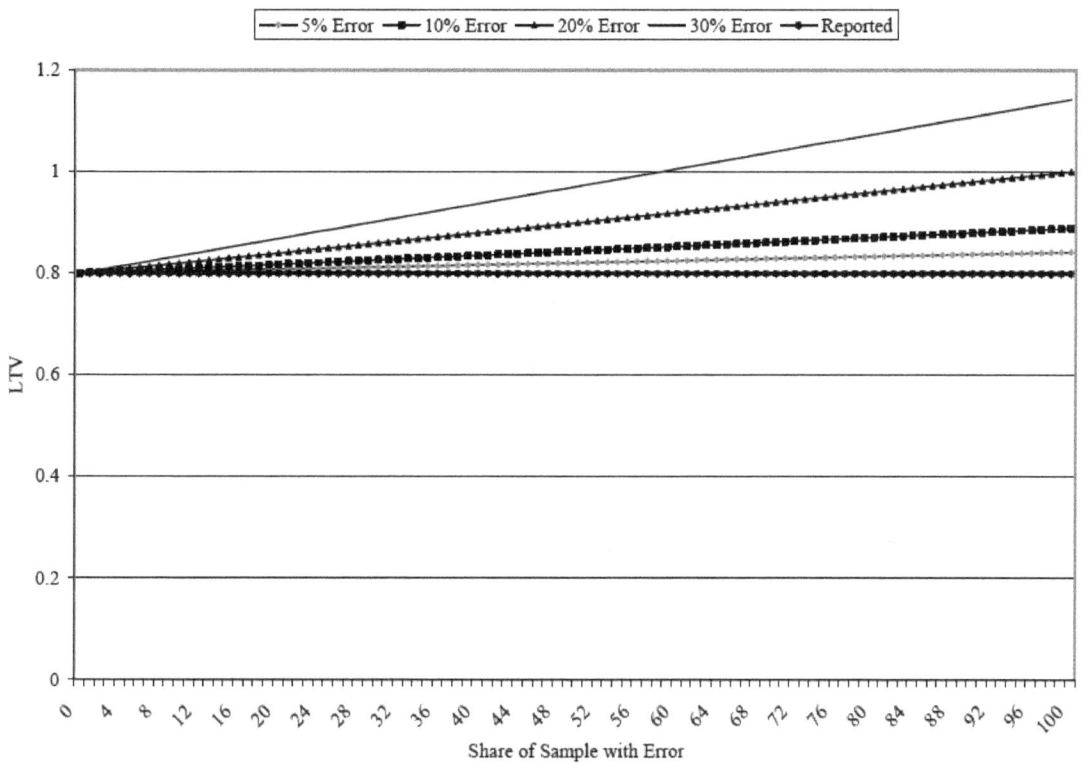

Appendix: Subprime Crisis Timeline[38]

March 2006—Median home prices fall 4.1 percent from fourth quarter of 2005 to first quarter of 2006.

May 2006—Merit Financial Corporation, a privately held mortgage company, files for bankruptcy.

December 28, 2006—Ownit Mortgage Solutions files for Chapter 11 bankruptcy.

February 5, 2007—Mortgage Lenders Network USA files for Chapter 11 bankruptcy.

March 2, 2007—New Century Financial Corporation, 2006's second-largest subprime lender with $51.6 billion in subprime loans, stops accepting new loan applications and files a Form 8-K with the SEC stating that it has $70 million in outstanding margin calls from five lenders and that its lenders are refusing access to financing.

April 3, 2007—New Century Financial Corporation files for Chapter 11 bankruptcy.

June 22, 2007—Bear Stearns announces that it is shoring up its High-Grade Structured Credit Fund with $3.2 billion and seeks help for its High-Grade Structured Credit Enhanced Leveraged Fund. The funds were invested in collateralized debt obligations backed by subprime mortgages.

July 10, 2007—Credit rating agencies downgrade hundreds of mortgage-backed securities. S&P places 612 U.S. subprime residential mortgage-backed securities, amounting to $7.4 billion in rated securities, on credit watch with negative implications.

July 31, 2007—Bear Stearns High-Grade Structured Credit Fund and the Bear Stearns High-Grade Structured Credit Enhanced Leveraged Fund file for bankruptcy after losing approximately $1.6 billion in investor capital.

August 2, 2007—American Home Mortgage Investment Corporation, the 12th-largest residential mortgage originator in 2006 with $58.9 billion in originations, announces it is filing for bankruptcy.

August 9, 2007—BNP Paribas suspends three investment funds that invest in subprime mortgage debt.

August 16, 2007—Countrywide Financial Corporation draws down its entire $11.5 billion credit line from a group of banks.

---

[38] In assembling this timeline, the following resources were helpful: Engen (2008), "The Financial Crisis" timeline of the Federal Reserve Bank of St. Louis (http://timeline.stlouisfed.org.)

September 13, 2007—British mortgage lender Northern Rock seeks emergency financial support from the Bank of England.

September 18, 2007—The Federal Reserve begins to lower interest rates.

October 24, 2007—Merrill Lynch announces an $8.4 billion loss and the departure of Chief Executive Officer Stanley O'Neal.

November 4, 2007—Citigroup announces that write-downs will amount to between $8 billion and $11 billion, and Charles Prince resigns as the bank's chief executive officer.

December 10, 2007—The Swiss bank UBS announces a $10 billion write-down for losses tied to mortgage-backed securities.

December 19, 2007—MBIA announces a $30 billion exposure to complex mortgage securities.

January 11, 2008—Bank of America announces that it will pay $4 billion to acquire Countrywide Financial.

February 17, 2008—The British government announces its takeover of Northern Rock.

March 11, 2008—The Federal Reserve Board announces the creation of the Term Securities Lending Facility, which may lend up to $200 billion of Treasury securities against federal agency debt; federal agency residential mortgage-backed securities; non-agency AAA-rated, private-label, residential mortgage-backed securities; and other securities. The Federal Open Market Committee increases its swap lines (liquidity enhancing reciprocal currency arrangements between central banks) with the European Central Bank and the Swiss National Bank and extends these lines through September 30, 2008.

March 16, 2008—Bear Stearns is reported to be acquired for $2 a share (later revised to approximately $9 a share) by JPMorgan Chase. The Federal Reserve assumes $30 billion in Bear Stearns assets. The Federal Reserve Board establishes the Primary Dealer Credit Facility to extend credit to primary dealers against a broad range of investment-grade securities.

May 2, 2008—The Federal Open Market Committee expands the list of eligible collateral for Term Securities Lending Facility auctions to include AAA-rated, asset-backed securities.

June 5, 2008—S&P downgrades monoline bond insurers AMBAC and MBIA from AAA to AA.

July 11, 2008—IndyMac Bank is placed into receivership by the FDIC.

August 7, 2008—Citigroup and Merrill Lynch agree to buy back $17.3 billion in auction-rate securities.

August 15, 2008—*Financial Times* reports that auction-rate security buybacks top $48 billion.

September 7, 2008—The U.S. government takes over Fannie Mae and Freddie Mac, replacing the management of the companies and providing up to $100 billion in capital for each company.

September 10, 2008—Lehman Brothers posts a $3.9 billion loss.

September 14, 2008—Bank of America buys Merrill Lynch. The Federal Reserve Board announces several initiatives to provide additional support to financial markets, including a significant broadening of collateral accepted by the Primary Dealer Credit Facility and the Term Securities Lending Facility.

September 15, 2008—Lehman Brothers files for bankruptcy.

September 16, 2008—Moody's and S&P downgrade ratings on AIG's credit. The U.S. government rescues AIG with an $85 billion loan through the Federal Reserve Bank of New York.

September 18, 2008—The SEC issues an emergency order that temporarily prohibits short sales in the securities of approximately 800 financial firms. The Federal Reserve announces the expansion of its swap lines with other central banks to address elevated pressures in funding markets.

September 19, 2008—The Federal Reserve Board announces that it is creating the Asset-Backed Commercial Paper Money Market Mutual Fund Liquidity Facility to extend nonrecourse loans to U.S. depository institutions to purchase asset-backed commercial paper from money market mutual funds. The Federal Reserve also announced that the Open Market Trading Desk will begin purchasing short-term debt obligations issued by Fannie Mae, Freddie Mac, and Federal Home Loan Banks.

September 22, 2008—Morgan Stanley and Goldman Sachs convert to commercial banks, and New York State announces it will regulate part of the CDS market.

September 25, 2008—The FDIC seizes Washington Mutual, and its banking assets are sold to JPMorgan Chase for $1.9 billion.

September 29, 2008—The FDIC announces that Citigroup will acquire the banking assets of Wachovia.

September 30, 2008—The SEC and the Financial Accounting Standards Board provide additional guidance on the interpretation of the mark-to-market accounting rule.

October 3, 2008—President George W. Bush signs into law the Emergency Economic Stabilization Act of 2008, creating the $700 billion Troubled Assets Relief Program (TARP). Wells Fargo makes a higher offer than Citigroup for all of Wachovia's assets, eventually winning the deal.

October 6, 2008—An ISDA auction values Fannie Mae and Freddie Mac debt at 91.51 percent.

October 7, 2008—The Federal Reserve Board announces the creation of the Commercial Paper Funding Facility to purchase three-month unsecured and asset-backed commercial paper from eligible issuers. The FDIC announces an increase in deposit insurance coverage to $250,000 per depositor (per bank).

October 14, 2008—The Treasury Department announces that the TARP will inject $250 billion into U.S. financial institutions. The FDIC expands guarantees to senior debt of all FDIC-insured financial institutions.

October 21, 2008—The Federal Reserve announces the creation of the Money Market Investor Funding Facility to provide up to $540 billion to buy assets from money market mutual funds.

October 29, 2008—The Federal Reserve lowers the Fed Funds rate to 1.0 percent.

November 10, 2008—The Federal Reserve and the Treasury Department announce restructuring and expansion of financial support for AIG.

November 13, 2008—The federal banking agencies announce proposed real estate appraisal and evaluation guidelines.

November 14, 2008—Freddie Mac posts loss of $25.3 billion.

November 17, 2008—Citigroup announces 50,000 job cuts.

November 23, 2008—The Federal Reserve, the Treasury Department, and the FDIC announce a rescue plan for Citigroup, including guarantees against unusually large losses in a $306 billion pool of assets and a capital infusion of $20 billion from the TARP fund.

November 25, 2008—The Federal Reserve announces the creation of the Term Asset-Backed Securities Loan Facility through the Federal Reserve Bank of New York to lend up to $200 billion on a nonrecourse basis to holders of AAA-rated asset-backed securities backed by consumer and small business loans. The Federal Reserve also announces the creation of a program to purchase the direct obligations of Fannie Mae, Freddie Mac, and the Federal Home Loan Banks and mortgage-backed securities backed by Fannie Mae, Freddie Mac, and Ginnie Mae.

December 1, 2008—National Bureau of Economic Research states that recession began in December 2007.

December 13, 2008—A $50 billion pyramid (Ponzi) scheme by Bernard Madoff is revealed.

January 16, 2009—The Treasury Department, the Federal Reserve, and the FDIC provide assistance to Bank of America, including guarantees against unusually large losses in a $118 billion pool of assets and a capital infusion of $20 billion from the TARP fund.